Is There Salvation Outside the Catholic Church?

AN AUTHORIZED TRANSLATION
FROM THE FRENCH OF
REV. J. BAINVEL, S.J.

BY
THE REV. J. L. WEIDENHAN, S.T.L.

SECOND EDITION

TAN BOOKS AND PUBLISHERS, INC.
Rockford, Illinois 61105

NIHIL OBSTAT

Sti. Ludovici, die 31 Maii, 1917.
F. G. Holweck,
Censor Librorum

IMPRIMATUR

Sti. Ludovici, die 6 Junii, 1917.
✠*Joannes J. Glennon,*
Archiepiscopus
Sti. Ludovici

TAN BOOKS AND PUBLISHERS, INC.
P. O. Box 424
Rockford, Illinois 61105
1979

PREFACE

To many the axiom " Outside the Church there is no salvation " has proven a veritable bugbear. From the days of Voltaire and J. J. Rousseau down to our own day, it has been the fruitful cause of innumerable taunts and sneers. Many denounce this barbarous — so they term it — survival of the Middle Ages, when not only heretics were burned, but every one who knowingly or unknowingly believed otherwise than the Roman Catholic and Apostolic Church, was pitilessly damned. Moreover, many Catholics of our own times, even those whose faith is not shaken, at least experience a certain uneasiness regarding their beliefs or in their relations with unbelievers, as soon as the trend of their thoughts or conversation bears on this subject. Many there are who wish, though they do not openly avow it, that the Catholic Church would be silent on this point and allow this dogma — since it really is a dogma — peacefully to slumber in the old

Latin tomes, unmolested and undisturbed.

Yet, if Catholics prefer not to discuss it, the same cannot be said of non-Catholics. They insist in bringing it to our attention, and, consequently, Catholic apologists are compelled to reply to their attacks.

Many of our apologists, it must be confessed, take the subject rather lightly. They imagine they have said the last word in the matter when they have established a clear-cut distinction between the body and the soul of the Church. Indeed, they feel no misgiving in declaring that it is quite sufficient for salvation to be a member of the soul of the Church. They do not see that the mighty axiom, as traditionally interpreted, insists, as we shall see later, on communion with the body of the Church as indispensably necessary. Their adversaries, provided they have a little knowledge of the question at issue, could easily show them the fallacy of their reasoning, not only by referring them back to the Fathers, but also by a direct appeal to the conclusions of the best theologians of more recent date, and also to the official and authoritative decisions of the Popes from Gregory XVI and

Pius IX down to Leo XIII and Pius X. Under such an appeal the apologist is forced to adopt one of two positions. He must either abandon the old dogmas which still obtain in Catholic theology and teaching, or he must adopt an interpretation alien to Christian tradition. This latter course is repugnant to Catholic thought.

Moreover, we are confronted with the disconcerting fact that theologians themselves are not agreed as to the manner of explaining this embarrassing axiom. Not a few are satisfied with the solution offered by the apologists above referred to, a solution which, however, we must consider inadequate.

It is fitting then, amidst this chaos, to direct our attention anew to the axiom and to the doctrine of which it is the official formula. Such a study will be doubly advantageous. First, it will help the reader to form more precise and perhaps more exact ideas regarding an important point of Catholic doctrine. It will help him to give a good account of it to himself, and whenever the need arises, to others. In the second place, it will help those to whom such questions appeal to understand the relation between revealed truths and their official *formulæ*, between dogma and theology, as also between the data of faith and their theological systematization.

CONTENTS

Contents

CONTENTS

IS THERE SALVATION OUTSIDE THE CATHOLIC CHURCH?

I

Notions and definitions. The body of the Church and the soul of the Church. Membership in the Church twofold: real and actual membership and membership by desire. Necessity of means and necessity of precept. Means absolutely necessary, and means necessary yet capable of supplements and equivalents.

In order to aid the reader in forming a correct idea of the many technical expressions which appear in this essay, it will be well, before entering into a detailed discussion of our subject, to recall a few necessary definitions.

When we speak of the *Body of the Church*

we mean the congregation of the faithful united by the profession of the same faith, participation in the same sacraments, and submission to the same lawful pastors with the sole purpose of serving God and obtaining salvation by employing the means prescribed by our Lord Jesus Christ, the divine Founder of the Church. In other words, the Body of the Church is the visible society established by Jesus Christ, the hierarchical organism within which He incorporated the religion which He had come upon earth to found. This body, be it understood, is not a dead body without a soul.

According to the most common definition, the *Soul of the Church* is the collection of those supernatural prerogatives with which our divine Lord has deigned to enrich His Church. Briefly stated, these are: the gift of truth attached to her infallible teaching; the gift of holiness inherent in her sacraments, her sacrifice, her liturgical prayers, etc.; infallibility promised to her official teaching body; and indefectibility guaranteed to her character of holiness, unity, and catholicity. As these gifts are communicated to her by the Holy Ghost, who is present in this great social body as its vivifying principle in precisely the same manner as the human soul informs our bodies with life, the Holy Ghost is often called the soul of the Church. We do not, however, understand the expression in this sense in our study. Sometimes we hear it said that the just are the soul of the Church, because they alone are in possession of sanctifying grace, which is the first principle of the supernatural life in the members of this social body, that is, the Church. It is in this sense that the expression — *to belong to the soul of the Church* — is usually explained.

When we speak of *membership in the Church*, without any further qualification, we are generally understood to refer to the body of the Church, or, what amounts to the same thing, to the visible Church. This alone, correctly speaking, forms a social body. To belong to the Church, then, is to be a member of the visible Church or the body of the Church.

We belong to the Church really and in fact (*re*) when we actually form part of this great social body. To that end we must have been initiated into it through baptism.

Besides we must not have abandoned it by apostasy or by the profession of heresy or schism, nor must we have been cut off from it by major excommunication. We belong to it by desire (*voto*), when, though not members in the proper meaning of the term, we nevertheless desire to be such. This desire may be explicit, as was the case with the catechumens of the early centuries. Likewise it may be implicit, as in the case of those who are unaware that there is a divinely founded Church, yet desire to do all that God requires of them for salvation. As we go along, we shall see how this desire to do all that God demands, really embodies the implicit wish to belong to the Church.

Further, membership in the Church may be regarded as necessary for salvation by *necessity of precept* or by *necessity of means*. It is necessary by a simple necessity of precept, if the sole reason for membership rests on a divine command, and if the disobedience to this command would mean the commission of a mortal sin, a state which directly precludes salvation. On the other hand, if God has entrusted His Church with all the means of salvation and constituted her the custodian of the keys of heaven, or if, (which amounts to the same thing), there is no entrance into the heavenly kingdom except the portals of the Church, nor any participation in the celestial gifts, save through and in the Church, then membership in it is necessary by *necessity of means*.

In the first case, whatever cause there might be, to lift the obligation of the precept would also render its observance unnecessary for salvation; in the second case, either ignorance of the means or the impossibility of employing these means certainly would relieve one of all fault, and hence, from liability to punishment. Nevertheless such ignorance or impossibility would prevent the realization of the end of man's creation, unless God in His mercy substituted some extraordinary means, just as whether by his own fault or not, no one can subsist without nourishment, save by a miracle.

There are some means of salvation so necessary for the attainment of our last end that no substitute can take their place, which means that they are absolutely necessary. Certainly no one is saved who dies in enmity with God; no one is saved who dies in unrepented personal sin; no one is saved without faith.   Other requirements are necessary by reason of the positive will of God.   In themselves these latter requisites are not absolutely necessary. God, their Author, reserves to Himself the right to substitute to them other means or to be satisfied with equivalent acts, in the case of those who, without any fault of their own, are unable to employ the divinely appointed means of salvation.   At first sight it would appear that the means set down are not necessary.   Nor are they, absolutely or strictly, taken in themselves.   Yet God regards them so, for the supplementary and equivalent acts only obtain value in the divine scheme of things in so far as they in some manner *represent* the means constituted and proclaimed necessary.

The natural course of human affairs or the analogies furnished by the ordinary workings of divine Providence enable us to determine in some measure whether a certain means is or is not necessary, or whether it is or is not rigorously required.   Strictly speaking such knowledge can be gleaned only from the revelation which God has vouch-safed to man. Consequently, in order to have correct ideas on these points, we must have recourse to revelation.

II

Two series of texts which are apparently contradictory. On the one hand we have a set which declares that out of the visible Church or the body of the Church there is no salvation; on the other hand, there are others which assure us that every man can be saved if he wills

The documents of revelation in the present case seem to create some slight difficulty. In point of fact, they yield us two apparently contradictory series of texts. One set informs us that there is no salvation outside the visible Church, that is, the body of the Church; the other affirms that every man can attain salvation if he wishes.

The dogma expressed in the formula at present under discussion, is immediately connected with a number of truths which lie at the basis of the Christian religion. It is not incumbent on us to prove these truths here.

8

That is done in theological treatises on the *Incarnation,* the *Redemption, Faith,* and the *Church.* It is sufficient for our present purpose briefly to recall them.

No one is saved except in Jesus and through Jesus, as St. Peter told the Sanhedrin after the cure of the paralytic.[1] To participate in the merits of Jesus and in the fruits of the Redemption, faith in Jesus is necessary: "He that believeth not shall be condemned."[2] Yet this faith by itself and alone cannot and does not suffice; it must, to be effective, be accompanied by sorrow for sin together with charity and good works.[3]

Yet even these taken together are inadequate for salvation in Jesus. Something else is also necessary, namely, baptism, the sacrament of faith and regeneration which incorporates us with Jesus by initiating us

[1] Acts VII. 11, 12: "Neither is there salvation in any other. For there is no other name under heaven given to men whereby we may be saved." Cf. Acts III. 23.

[2] Mark XVI. 16. Cf. Acts XIII. 48: "And as many as were ordained to life everlasting, believed."

[3] Acts III. 19: "Be penitent, therefore, and be converted, that your sins may be blotted out." Cf. James II. 14: "What shall it profit my brethren, if a man say he hath faith and have not works?" See also James III. 26.

into His Church. To Nicodemus, Jesus said: "Unless a man is born again of water and the Holy Ghost, he cannot enter into the kingdom of God." [4]   Again, before ascending into heaven, He commissioned His disciples to baptize all and at the same time to teach all: "Teach ye all nations and baptize them." [5]   For this reason the Apostles, after the great miracle of Pentecost, at once baptized all believers, for baptism was the rite of initiation into the new society — the society of salvation — securely and firmly founded on faith in Jesus.[6]   As is easily perceived, for the Apostles and the early faithful, incorporation with Jesus and incorporation into His mystical body — the Church — were one and the same thing. This is the keynote of St. Paul's preaching, and he constantly refers to it in his Epistles.[7]

From these various statements we may

[4] John III. 5.

[5] Matt. XXVIII. 18, 19.

[6] Acts II. 41: "They that received this word were baptized." See Acts VIII. 36–38: "As they went on their way they came to a certain water; and the eunuch said: See, here is water, what doth hinder me from being baptized?"

[7] See I Cor. XII. 27; Eph. I. 23; IV. 11–16; V. 24, 30; Coloss. I. 18.

rightly conclude that in the early stages of Christian thought the Church was as necessary for salvation as Christ Himself. In his First Epistle, St. Peter had instituted a comparison — destined to become classical in Christian tradition — between the Church and Noe's ark. As the inmates of the ark were the sole survivors of the deluge, so only those who have entered the Church through baptism will gain eternal salvation.[8] This is why the early Christians delighted in comparing themselves to shipwrecked mariners mercifully rescued by Christ's bark — the Church — whilst they regarded the rest of mankind as lost in the great cataclysm to which the human race was doomed. For them, the Church was the society of the elect, the society of the saved, or, to be more accurate, the society of salvation.[9]

[8] See I Pet. III. 20–21 and the context.

[9] See Acts II. 47; I Cor. I. 18; 2 Cor. II. 15. This does not mean that the early Christians regarded the elect as the only members of the Church; nor does it mean that only those who were admitted to her bosom through baptism were assured of salvation. What we wish to emphasize in these texts is the assurance which was felt by those within the bark of the Church, whilst the rest of mankind who had not come within the pale of the Church

The same doctrine is expressed by the holy
Fathers but under widely different aspects.
St. Irenæus declares that " where the Church
is, there is the spirit of God, and where the
spirit of God is, there is the Church and every
kind of grace." [10]   For Irenæus then, only
those possess the spirit of Christ, that is,

---

were looked upon as lost forever. They were deeply
conscious of the fact that their bark would unfail-
ingly bring them to port and they gave little thought
to the possibility of their own rejection before the
haven of safety was reached.

[10] *Treatise against Heresies,* bk. III. c. xxiv, no. 1.
The same idea runs through the whole context.
Speaking of faith, he says we have received it from
the Church. "For this gift of God," he adds, "has
been entrusted to the Church, as breath was to the
first created man, for this purpose, that all the members receiving it, may be vivified; to it has been communicated the gift of Christ, that is, the Holy Spirit,
the earnest of incorruption, the means of confirm-
ing our faith and the ladder of ascent to God. For
in the Church, St. Paul tells us, God hath set apostles,
prophets, teachers and all other means through
which the Spirit works; of which all those are not
partakers who do not join themselves to the Church,
but defraud themselves of life." Then follows the
sentence quoted above in the text. Irenæus con-
cludes: "Those, therefore, who do not partake of
the Spirit, are not nourished into life from the
mother's breasts." Passages of a similar import
abound in his writings.

have the supernatural life, who are affiliated with the Church. Again, he expresses the same idea when he tells us that " the Apostles, like a rich man depositing his money in the bank, lodged in her (the Church's) hands most copiously all things pertaining to the truth; so that every man, whoever will, can draw from her the water of life. For she is the entrance to life." [11] Which, in other language, means that affiliation with the Church is necessary before any one can share in her riches. St. Cyprian gives expression to the same truth in language even more forcible — if such were possible — in his *Treatise on the Unity of the Church*. We will merely content ourselves with recalling his famous utterance, which sums up all the others on this point, " No one can have God for his father, who has not the Church for his mother." [12]

Christian tradition has never wearied in repeating and emphasizing this teaching. It is found in the definitions of the Councils, in the prayers of the liturgy, in the theological theses bearing on the necessity of communion

[11] *Treatise against Heresies*, bk. III, c. iv, no. 1.
[12] No. 6.

with the Church, in the sermons of the
Church preachers, and lastly in the religious
consciousness of the faithful.   True it is that
many of the ordinary faithful had rather
hazy and inexact ideas in regard to the salvation of unbelievers as also the condition of
children dying without baptism; yet all of
them knew, and all of them insisted, that
there is no salvation except in the Church of
Christ.[13]

[13] Here are a few extracts culled from many
sources, which we give not so much to prove the mind
of the Church on this point (for this is self-evident)
as to show how and in what way she expresses it.
Writing to the schismatical bishops, Pope Pelagius II
declares: "Whosoever will not remain within the
peace and unity of the Church, will not possess the
Saviour." *Enchiridion,* Denzinger-Bannwart (EDB).
11th ed. 1911, no. 246. In 1208, Pope Innocent III
obliged the converted Waldenses to make a profession of faith in which was embodied this phrase:
"We believe in our hearts and we confess with our
lips one and one only Church, not the Church of the
heretics, but the Roman, Holy, Catholic and Apostolic Church, out of which no one can be saved"
(EDB 423). In 1215, under the same Pope, the
Fourth Lateran Council defined that "there is only
one universal Church of the faithful, outside of
which absolutely no one is saved" (EDB 430).
A similar assertion is found in the famous bull
Unam sanctam of Boniface VIII (1302), where we

Their language leaves no room for doubt that it is the visible Church they have in mind. There can be no mistake that they

find also allusions to the ark of Noe. EDB 468. In the same bull, the final definition (for it is, despite what may be said to the contrary, a true definition *ex cathedra*) is even more to the point, in this that it reduces the whole question to one of submission to the Roman Pontiff. " We declare, assert, define and pronounce that submission to the Roman Pontiff is necessary for every human being who wishes to be saved." EDB 469. The statements of the Council of Florence embodied in the decree for the Jacobites (1441) are, if we may use the expression, more insistent still. " The holy Roman Church . . . firmly believes, professes, and preaches that any one who is not within the fold of the Catholic Church, not only pagans, but Jews, heretics, and schismatics can have no share in the life eternal . . . unless before death they become affiliated with her; and that so important is the unity of this ecclesiastical body that only those who remain within its pale can profit by the sacraments of the Church unto salvation, and they alone can receive an eternal recompense for their fasts, their alms-giving, their other works of Christian devotion, and the ordinary duties of the Christian soldier. No one, let his almsgiving be as great as it may, no one, even if he pour out his blood for the name of Christ, can be saved if he does not remain within the bosom and the unity of the Catholic Church." EDB 714.

We might add to the statements of St. Irenæus and St. Cyprian, already quoted, any number of

are referring to that very Church, entrance
into which is gained only by baptism, that
Church, affiliation with which is lost by a
lapse into heresy or schism, that Church
based on hierarchical authority, in which, to
use the phrase of St. Ignatius of Antioch,
the bishop must be obeyed even as Christ
Himself, that Church, finally, which the

others bearing the same import. Suffice it to men-
tion a few of the most striking. Origen declares:
"Let no one be deceived: outside this building, that
is the Church, no one is saved. If any one leave
it, he is responsible for his own death" (*In Jesu
Nave,* hom. 3, n. 5). St. Jerome (Epist. 15, *ad
Damasum,* n. 2) writes: "This is the house
where alone the paschal lamb can be rightly eaten.
If one is not within the ark of Noe, he will
perish in the deluge." St. Augustine says: "He
(Emeritus) cannot attain to salvation except in the
Catholic Church. Outside the Catholic Church, he
can do everything but be saved. He can have hon-
ors, he can partake of the sacrament, but nowhere
except in the Catholic Church will he be able to
find salvation" (*Sermo ad Caesariensis Ecclesiae ple-
bem,* no. 6). It is useless to multiply examples, for although expressed in various forms, the underlying
thought is always the same. The Fathers do not
touch on the question of good faith and invincible
ignorance, but they affirm, with all possible emphasis,
the necessity of communion with the Church for
salvation.

Fathers expressly designate as the Catholic, Apostolic, Roman Church.

The Vatican Council did not define this doctrine; most likely it would have done so, had there been time, for it is mentioned explicitly in the rough draft of the constitution entitled *De Ecclesia Christi* (The Church of Christ) which was proposed to the deliberations of the Council. Still Pius IX, in a prior document, had already qualified this teaching as a Catholic dogma.[14]

[14] In his allocution *Singulari nos,* dated Dec. 9, 1854, the day after he had solemnly defined the dogma of the Immaculate Conception, the Pope declared: "Another and no less pernicious error (than Rationalism) has made itself felt within certain portions of the Catholic world — a fact the . . . of which knowledge pains us greatly — and it has fixed itself in the convictions of a goodly number of Catholics. They maintain that those who abide not in the true Church of Christ can hope for eternal salvation. . . . It is our apostolic duty to excite your solicitude and your episcopal vigilance so that with all your energy, you may take means to eradicate from the minds of men this impious and baneful opinion which declares that the way of salvation can be found through all religions. . . . It must be held as an article of faith that out of the Apostolic Roman Church no one can be saved, for she is the one and only ark of salvation, which unless one gain entrance into, he must perish in the deluge."

Consequently, it is a dogma of our faith that out of the Church there is no salvation, and by " Church " is meant the visible and hierarchical Church, the Roman Catholic Church.[15]

Over against all the data we have thus far adduced, we have the explicit teaching of St. Paul that God desires the salvation of the whole world.[16]   One of the teachings which

EDB 1646–1647. In his encyclical *Quanto conficia-mur,* dated August 10, 1863, Pius calls this teaching a " Catholic dogma." EDB 1677.

[15] The official documents of the Church and the patristic evidence on this question may be found in the theological treatises on the Church. See for example the *De Ecclesia Christi* of Cardinal Billot, vol. I, 3rd ed. Thesis II, p. 101–122. For the official documents of the Church, see also the *Enchiridion symbolorum* of Denzinger-Bannwart, 11th ed. 1911, *Index systematicus,* under the word, *Ecclesia,* under the caption: *Est omnibus ad salutem necessaria, " extra quam nulla salus" nec remissio peccatorum.* For the patristic testimony, see the *Enchiridion* of Rouet de Journel, 1911, *Index theologicus,* no. 47.

[16] I Tim. II. 4. The Church has condemned the following Jansenistic proposition: " It is semi-Pelagian doctrine to say that Christ died for all men and shed His blood for all " (EDB 1096). The proposition in whole, is condemned " as false, presumptuous, scandalous, and, understood in the sense that Christ did not die but for the elect, as heretical."

the Church holds as certain, is that no one is lost except through his own fault, that God will not fail us, if we do not fail Him, that no one is held responsible in His sight for a duty whose fulfilment is rendered impossible by invincible ignorance. The Church even goes farther. No Catholic denies, nor can he deny without running counter to the Church's teaching, that among Protestants, schismatics and pagans there are souls which are really on the road to eternal life.[17]

It appears, however, that the same recognition was not always given this second series of truths, nor were they as insistently professed by the faithful at large, as was the doctrine which emphasized the necessity of the Church for salvation. Indeed many instances could be given in which even well in-

---

[17] Pius IX teaches this directly or indirectly in his encyclical of Aug. 10, 1863: "We all know that those who are invincibly ignorant of our religion and who nevertheless lead an honest and upright life, can, under the influence of divine light and divine grace, attain to eternal life; for God who knows and sees the mind, the heart, the thoughts, and the dispositions of every man, cannot in His infinite bounty and clemency permit any one to suffer eternal punishment who is not guilty through his own fault." EDB 1677.

structed Catholics attributed to the Church
a teaching directly the contrary.[18] Yet
the Church herself never lost sight of the
divine intention to save the whole world, nor
did she ever cease to teach that the graces of
salvation were ever possible to the souls filled
with good will. Nay more, she has always
consistently maintained that no one is
damned except through his own fault. All
ecclesiastical writers, and this is especially
true of the Greeks, are one in claiming that
the light diffused by the divine Word has always shone and will continue to shine not
only upon the children of God within the
Church but also upon those beyond her pale.
Even St. Augustine, who, as is well known,

[18] This is well instanced by the example of Xavier
de Maistre who was fully convinced that his loyalty
to the Church demanded that he regard his wife
Sophie, a woman of angelic virtue, as doomed to damnation if she remained a schismatic. But he refused
to concede the possibility of such a fate for her.
His strange belief he attributed to a Catholic priest
whom he had consulted regarding the matter. His
error lay in the fact that he had concerned himself
little with further investigation, for doubtless he had
not understood the priest rightly. See *Lettres in-
édites de Xavier de Maistre à sa famille,* published
by Rev. F. Klein in the *Correspondant,* Dec. 25, 1902,
p. 1109–1110.

is particularly hard upon heretics and unbelievers, does not hesitate in his controversy with the Pelagians, to concede that in the eyes of men there are many souls apparently outside the Church, who in reality are within her fold in the sight of God.[19] He likewise admits that God, in a manner peculiar to Himself, and in a way beyond our finite understanding, acts upon these souls, enlightens them, and saves them without the ordinary economy of salvation, which is affiliation with the Church.[20]

We are, then, confronted by two series of texts and statements which on their face appear to be contradictory. On the one hand, we have the necessity of means positively instituted by God and our Saviour Jesus Christ, a necessity so indispensable that no one can be saved unless he employs this means in practice. On the other hand, we have the

---

[19] In his *Treatise on Baptism* against the Donatists, bk. V, c. xxviii, no. 39: "When we speak of within and without in relation to the Church, it is the position of the heart that we must consider, not that of the body." He adds: "All who are within in heart are saved in the unity of the ark."

[20] *Treatise on the True Religion*, c. xxv, no. 46. The text will be given below.

excusing cause of invincible ignorance, the merciful bounty of God towards all men, and the fact that the graces of salvation are proffered to every man in such degree that the responsibility of his salvation rests entirely upon him and not upon God.[21]

This is the problem which must be met not only by the theologian but also by every Catholic who at all reflects on his faith and has its welfare at heart. The necessity of the Church for salvation is not really connected with the particular question under discussion. It presupposes the reception of baptism, faith in Jesus Christ, faith in a supernatural revelation, without which, according to the Epistle to the Hebrews, it is impossible to please God, and without which, according to the Vatican Council, it is impossible to be numbered among His children, since no one is ever justified without it.[22] Our task will be to examine what sort of affiliation with the Church is necessary for

[21] These phases of the question are brought out clearly by Pius IX in his allocution of 1854 and in his encyclical of 1863, to which we have referred above.

[22] Constitution *Dei Filius,* c. 3, EDB 1793.

salvation. Our conclusion on this point applies as well, within the restrictions laid down, to analogous questions and whatever modifications are bound up with them.

Evidently, the solution of the difficulty does not lie in the sacrifice of either of the apparently contradictory truths, nor in the rationalistic denial of the data of the problem. The true and only solution must and does rest on the reconciliation of the seemingly discordant teachings. Should it happen that this reconciliation is not as complete as we should like (as for instance in regard to the efficacy of grace and human liberty), we would not thereby be justified in rejecting a truth which the Church regards as certain. We must always bear in mind that our own knowledge is perforce very much limited, and we must concede that the workings of God surpass all understanding. Still, if we are unable to give a positive solution which will satisfy all parties and all points, we can, as it were, explain the difficulty at least negatively to the extent that there is no real contradiction between the two truths proposed for our belief.

Our first step, then, will be to view the

various solutions offered in explanation of the problem. This done, we will select the one which appears to be more in harmony with the principles of theology and reason, and at the same time responds best to all the data of the problem and which can best unite these data in one harmonious synthesis.

III

Inadequate solutions: good faith, the soul of the Church, the invisible Church, the necessity of precept

Many Catholics when confronted with the objections urged against their religion on this score, seem to think that they have explained away the difficulty by the assertion that good faith suffices for, and insures salvation. Yet such an explanation when examined closely demands the sacrifice of the positive data regarding the necessity of affiliation with the Church, and at the same time it opens wide the door to religious indifference. The Church has again and again combated such a tendency by emphasizing the traditional teaching and by repeatedly bringing to mind the axiom which we are discussing.[1]

But does this mean that the question of good faith has no bearing on the problem

[1] See the documents of Pius IX to which we have referred.

at all? By no means. Pius IX, in the documents cited, refers expressly to the excusing
cause of good faith and invincible ignorance.
" It must be equally held as certain, that
ignorance of the true faith, if it be invincible,
excuses one from all fault in the eyes of the
Saviour." [2]   " Not only does it relieve the
ignorant person from all punishment," but it
actually precludes it, " when he employs
other means, according to his capacity, in order to gain the grace of attaining eternal
life." [3]   There was never a time in the history of the Church when due credit was not
given to good faith as an excusing cause, but
formerly it was less insisted upon than it is
nowadays. Perhaps the fact that in earlier
days men relied more on truth and its con-
vincing power accounts for their refusal to
give that excusing cause due credit in
the sphere of religion. Then, men were
less preoccupied with the individual and the
inner workings of conscience, matters which
they left to God's judgment, than they were
with the outward and social conditions af-
fecting truth and its claims. And it was

[2] EDB 1647.
[3] EDB 1677.

this same tendency which urged the formulation of principles and theses, in which no account was taken of individual cases or particular eventualities or hypotheses. Furthermore, prudence demanded that they seek not to probe too deeply into the secret workings of conscience. "What a presumption it is," says Pius IX in his allocution of 1854, "to attempt to fix the limits of invincible ignorance (and consequently of good faith)! Let whatever credit is due good faith be given it, but let it not entail the slighting of truth and its claims."

As we have already indicated in the beginning of this essay, others meet the objections by distinguishing the body of the Church from the soul of the Church. They agree that affiliation with the soul of the Church is necessary for salvation, whereas that membership in the body of the Church is not necessary. Such an explanation is not entirely erroneous, for it does partly answer the difficulty. Still it is not a satisfactory solution of the problem. Our brethren of other faiths would have little difficulty in baring its weak points. They need but to point to the fact that taken in its traditional

sense, our axiom implied and still implies affiliation with the body of the Church.   And
on this point they certainly would be correct.
Furthermore, the solution offers no explanation of the exact relations of the soul of the
Church to the body of the Church; a point,
we fear, upon which our apologists are rather
hazy, usually sacrificing too much to the
claims of good faith.

Similarly, the solution which rests on the
distinction between the visible Church and
the invisible Church is open to the same embarrassing counter objections.   As a matter
of fact our axiom refers to the visible
Church, and until an adequate explanation is
given regarding the precise relations of the
visible Church to the invisible Church, the
solution must be regarded as unsatisfactory.

Some apologists, and among them are
numbered several theologians of note,[4] accept the distinction between the soul and
body of the Church, but supplement it by a
second distinction based on the necessity of
means and the necessity of precept.   Herein

---

[4] Among others we may mention Rev. E. Hugon
O. P., *Hors de l'Eglise point de salut*, Paris 1907.
See the Preface.

they approach very near the correct solution without actually arriving at it. In their system, the necessity of means admits neither dispensation nor exception. Whosoever fails to employ these means, whether culpably or inculpably, cannot attain the end in view. But with the necessity of precept the case is different, for here ignorance and impossibility form sufficient excuses.[5] They insist that affiliation with the soul of the Church is necessary for salvation by a necessity of means, but claim that membership in the body of the Church is necessary only by a necessity of precept. Consequently, no one can be saved who does not belong to the soul of the Church, but one can be saved without being affiliated with the body of the Church. In this case, as in others, the precept is binding only upon those who are cognizant of its existence and are in a position

[5] The reason of this difference is that when there is question of the necessity of means, the means have a positive and direct influence upon the attainment of the end, just as nourishment has the tendency to preserve life; when there is question of the necessity of precept, the act commanded or forbidden may in itself be indifferent to the end, or at least have no direct bearing upon its attainment.

to fulfil it. This solution, as we have re-
marked, has been accepted as adequate by
very distinguished theologians. Nevertheless it does not solve the difficulty.

First of all, it apparently is not consonant
with the traditional interpretation nor does
it harmonize sufficiently with the other theological data bound up with the difficulty.
When the holy Fathers speak of affiliation
with the Church as necessary for salvation,
their expressions are so sweeping and so
absolute that it is indeed difficult to make
them refer merely to a necessity of precept.
Very likely their dictum bore directly upon
souls who resisted the truth, or who obsti-
nately adhered to their private beliefs, or
who were blinded by passion. Still, they do
not speak of the necessity of the Church for
salvation in the same strain as they do of the
necessity of obeying the positive commands
of God. In some cases, it is true, they refer to the sin of apostasy, but in the ma-
jority of instances their expressions go much
farther than this. As a matter of fact they
go so far as to assert that even though a man
do all the good possible, he can scarcely be
saved if he be without the pale of the

Church. When their attention is brought to bear upon the case of those who through no fault of their own are not members of the Church, and still, aided by the grace of God, do all they can for salvation, they claim that such persons are members of the Church in heart and that God looks upon them as His own, even though they actually are among the enemies of His religion. Hence it is not a question of precept that they have in mind whenever they discuss the necessity of membership in the Church. Although they do not make the technical distinctions of theology, there is little difficulty in realizing that they regarded the Church as a necessary means of salvation. This is likewise the teaching of the more authoritative theologians. Nay more, this is the doctrine given as the traditional interpretation in the sketch of the chapter " on the constitution of the Church of Christ " which was proposed to the deliberations of the Vatican Council (1869–1870).[6]

[6] The sixth chapter of the sketch of this constitution was entitled, *The Church is a Society absolutely necessary for Salvation.* The chapter is well worth quoting here, because, in affirming expressly that affiliation with the Church is necessary by necessity of

True the draft did not receive official
sanction, and therefore has no authoritative
value; but the fact that the theologian re-
dactors of the draft proposed this doctrine,
clearly shows that they themselves regarded
it as the expression of the indisputable and
incontestable mind of the Church.   Is it not
the common teaching of theologians that

means, it gives at the same time the doctrinal bases
of the assertion and proposes them in the very language of Scripture. It reads: "Hinc omnes in-
telligant, quam necessaria ad salutem obtinendam
societas sit Ecclesia Christi. Tantae nimirum neces-
sitatis, quantae consortium et conjunctio est cum
Christo capite et mystico ejus corpore, praeter quod
nullam aliam communionem ipse nutrit et fovet
tanquam Ecclesiam suam, quam solam dilexit et
seipsum tradidit pro ea, ut illam sanctificaret, mun-
dans lavacro aquae in verbo vitae ut exhiberet ipse
sibi gloriosam Ecclesiam, non habentem maculam,
aut rugam, aut aliquid hujusmodi, sed ut sit sancta
et immaculata. Idcirco docemus, Ecclesiam non
liberam societatem esse, quasi indifferens sit ad
salutem, eam sive nosse sive ignorare, sive ingredi
sive relinquere; sed esse omnino necessariam et
quidem necessitate non tantum praecepti dominici
quo Salvator omnibus gentibus eam ingrediendam
praescripsit; verum etiam medii, quia in instituto
salutaris providentiae ordine, communicatio sancti
Spiritus, participatio veritatis et vitae non obtinetur,
nisi in Ecclesia et per Ecclesiam, cujus caput est
Christus."

baptism is necessary by a necessity of means, and is it not in order to reconcile this necessity of means with the certain fact that martyrdom insures salvation, without the reception of baptism of water, that the notion that the baptism of blood and the baptism of desire are substitutes for the baptism of water has been incorporated into Catholic teaching and has even found its way into our elementary catechisms? Hence, if baptism is necessary by a necessity of means, the Church must be equally necessary, for baptism is essentially incorporation with Jesus by incorporation in His Church — His mystical body. Therefore, it cannot be said that affiliation with the body of the Church is necessary only by a necessity of precept.

The same conclusion must be drawn concerning the Catholic teaching on the state of children dying without baptism. Certainly such infants are incapable of any precept, and still they are deprived of the happiness of heaven, because they have been unable to avail themselves of a necessary means. All theologians unhesitatingly subscribe to this doctrine, basing their acceptance on the words of Jesus to Nicodemus, "Unless a man be born again of water and the Holy Ghost, he cannot enter into the kingdom of God." As a consequence we may again conclude that membership in the body of the Church is not only necessary by a necessity of precept, but also by a necessity of means.

The same conclusion is reached by a close examination of the necessity of belonging to the soul of the Church, a necessity which these very theologians, whose position we are criticizing, admit is a necessity of means. What do they really mean by affiliation with the soul of the Church? Many of them who employ the term seem to have rather confused ideas as to its exact meaning. In their minds, to belong to the soul of the Church is to live the life of grace and to have faith and charity. But why do they claim that those who have faith and charity and live a life of grace are members of the soul of the Church? There is no reason at all to introduce this notion, if there is not an intrinsic and necessary relation in the concrete, between the supernatural life and the Church itself. They might reply perhaps that they use this form of expression in order to be in harmony with the old axiom which insists that outside the Church there is no salvation. But their explanation does not conform to the axiom, rather it denudes it of sense. They empty it of its real meaning when they refuse to admit the intrinsic and necessary relation between the life of grace and membership in the Church. In other terms, it is the visible Church, the ecclesiastical organism, which is the mystical body of Christ; it is this body which is animated by His Spirit. Just as the members of our body cannot receive the vital influx from the soul, unless they form a real part of this animated body, so no one can live the life of Christ and be animated with His spirit unless he belongs to His mystical body, which is the Church.[7] Briefly put, the soul of the Church bears a necessary relation to the body of the Church. The same conclusion is forced upon us by another line of argument. If affiliation with the soul of the Church is necessary by a

[7] This is the comparison employed by St. Augustine in speaking of the spiritual union with the body of Christ, and it seems he gives the same meaning which we are applying here. *In Joan.* tr. 27, no. 6.

necessity of means, then membership in the body of the Church must be necessary by the same necessity.

Not one of the solutions examined thus far is really satisfactory. Those which have the appearance of plausibility are found on closer examination to be merely clever evasions. True, they safeguard the words of our axiom, but only at the expense of the doctrine bound up with it. This doctrine they clothe in a phraseology so confused that, although it may dazzle, it can never convince the mind. Hence a satisfactory solution must be sought in another direction.

IV

THE SOLUTION OF THE PROBLEM LIES IN
THE FACT THAT WE CAN BE MEMBERS OF
THE CHURCH IN TWO WAYS, EXTERNALLY
(VISIBLY) AND INTERNALLY (INVISIBLY).
THIS, HOWEVER, NEEDS SOME EXPLANA-
TION.

This solution is by no means new, for it
was advocated by the old theologians, especially by St. Thomas.[1] True it is, that in
the beginning its elaboration was by no
means perfect, but as time went on, it was
gradually developed into perfection and into
doctrinal synthesis, but always *in eodem
sensu,* within the same meaning and always
in the light of the data afforded by the
Church Fathers. Before we go into any
detailed exposition, let us recall the data of

[1] See for example his *Summa,* part 3, qu. 68, art.
2, on baptism as a condition of salvation; see also
qu. 73, art. 3, on the Eucharist as a condition of
salvation.

the problem which we have collected in our examination of the various solutions we have discarded as inadequate.

According to the Catholic doctrine, to gain salvation, affiliation in some way with the body of the Church is necessary. Since the time of her establishment by Christ, union with the Church is obligatory upon all by necessity of means. On the other hand we know that faith and charity are sufficient to insure salvation. As every one must admit, there are many souls who, thanks to the saving designs of God, possess faith and charity without being affiliated with the body of the Church, in fact without knowing that there is such an institution as the true Church, and consequently, are so placed that they are incapable of union with her.

The contradiction, upon its statement, is clear to every one. But is it real? It would be if there were one and one only means of being united to the Church, either by an external and visible affiliation or by the soul's consciousness that it forms part of this body. But, as we know from Scripture, whose words St. Thomas insists on just on this very point, " men see the appearance of things, but God sees the inmost depths of the heart." As far as man can judge, many souls are apparently outside the pale of the Church, and yet these same souls in God's sight are united to the Church and are members of the mystical body of Jesus. Right here we must make a distinction between desire and reality, between the will and the fact, between internal affiliation with the Church and affiliation by the external ties of life and communion. The principle of the true solution of the problem is embodied in this distinction. But it may be — and is — that even among those who are somewhat familiar with the Church's teaching on this point, because of the constant repetition of a lesson learned in their catechism days, there are many who have not grasped the exact meaning, or assimilated the tremendous reality hidden under the formula. A clear exposition of the Church's teaching, then, will not be amiss.

When Jesus laid the foundation of His Church, He intended that from that very moment, it should be the sole economy of salvation. For just as no one can hope for salvation except through Him, so no one can be saved unless he become part of His mystical body.   Not only has He confided to the ·Church, or, to put it more correctly, deposited in her social conscience,[2] the sum of truths which must be believed; not only has He made her the dispensatrix of the sacramental graces, but over and above this, He desired that the mysterious action of His Spirit in the souls of men should not be exercised except in His mystical body — His Church.   It is then, in the Church and through the Church, that here on earth Jesus sanctifies the souls ransomed by His blood.   In order to participate in the divine life, we must, in God's sight, belong to the mystical body of Christ; souls are not incorporated with Christ except in the Church. This is a revealed truth of which account must be taken, if we would rightly understand the workings of Providence on the souls of men in the economy of salvation. It is this very truth which is formulated in the axiom, " Outside of the Church there is

[2] For a right understanding of this social conscience, see *La vie du dogme,* by A. de la Barre; see also Bainvel, *De Magisterio vivo et Traditione, passim,* but especially the second part, chap. I, no. 42.

no salvation." Every man, bound to live
the life of God by living the life of Jesus,
must as a consequence do his best to enter
the Church, the only organism in which
Christ's life courses. But for many souls,
this real entrance into the Church is impossible simply because they are not aware of
the existence of a Church, much less that
baptism is the rite by which incorporation
into this society is gained. Should they be
held responsible for their invincible ignorance? God might have allowed them to be
deprived of supernatural gifts without any
personal fault of theirs; for these gifts are
gratuitous and no one has a right to them.
Thus, He allows such deprivation in the case
of children dying without baptism, and
adults whose mental powers are too poorly
developed to enable them to live a truly
moral life. There is, according to the opinion of St. Augustine, for each soul in particular, a supernatural Providence insuring
graces which flow upon the soul independ-
ently of all ordinary channels; if such souls
are faithful to these graces, they will inevi-
tably, without any visible communion with
the Church and Christian preaching, come to

the knowledge of the sum of supernatural truths necessary to make the acts of faith and charity insuring salvation.

But is this not tantamount to saying that souls are saved outside the Church, and that therefore, our axiom, " Outside the Church there is not salvation," is not absolutely true? To this question two replies are possible, neither of which is opposed to the other. By uniting them we obtain a theological solution of the problem which reconciles all the facts of the case.

V

First of all, the axiom may be understood as referring to the ordinary workings of Providence, that is to say, it is the rule and not the exception. It is indeed the order desired by God, the rule He lays down, that all shall be saved within the Church. The exceptional cases, be they ever so numerous — and they are less numerous than appears at first sight — are outside the divine intention (praeter intentionem, per accidens) because of the fault of the human will, and are supplied by God with an extraordinary economy, a special Providence, granted in the measure of necessity. That they live in the Church cannot be doubted, but they do not live in it fully.

As a preliminary remark, we may state — and this is the explanation of St. Augustine, put, however, into more exact terms — that our axiom must be understood to refer to the ordinary economy of Providence, to the usual order of things, or to use the term of Mgr. d'Hulst, to the official economy. It makes no pretence to, nor does it actually embrace the exceptional cases which are outside the usual order of God's ways, and depend exclusively on those mysterious laws of the divine action in the soul of each man, laws which God has not deigned to reveal (except as they are summed up in the general principle of His all-saving will), and as a consequence, laws which the Church has not imposed for our belief by a doctrinal definition.[1]

[1] See the passage of St. Augustine to which allusion is made in our study. It is taken from his treatise on the *True Religion*, c. 25, no. 46, and reads: "Divine Providence is concerned with men individually as well as with mankind taken collectively; what God does for each man in particular He Himself knows and they in whom He does it, what He does for mankind is manifested in history and prophecy." Billot quotes this very text and comments upon it, *op. cit.*, pp. 121–122. Still it can be said also that in many cases those in whom God acts have but an imperfect knowledge of that divine action: they experience the action of grace without knowing whence it comes or whither it goeth.

When the Church insists that outside her pale there is no salvation, she does not intend thereby to pass judgment on individual cases, nor on the exceptions to the rule, nor on whatever, to employ the language of philosophy, is connected *per accidens* (by accident) with the general economy of salvation. What she does mean to say is that the Church is essentially *the* society of salvation, and that there is none other, for he who desires eternal life must enter her fold. And God has established the Church in the world with such marks of her divine mission, with such a miraculous means of propagation, ornate with such effulgence, that, according to the normal course of things, provided man does not blind himself to the truth and its salutary influence, or screen its light from reaching others, every man is given the opportunity of knowing the Church and her divine institution. All who fail to gain this knowledge have no one to blame but themselves. Therefore, in the order of Providence no one can be saved without entering the Church.

But God has willed that the realization of this providential order should depend partly

on the human will. By refusing knowingly
to cooperate with His designs, by resisting
His grace, by opposing the efficaciousness of
the means which He has established, man
has the awful privilege, not only to shut his
eyes to the light and close his ears to the
whisperings of grace, but also to prevent the
light shining for others and to thwart the
right understanding of the divine appeals.
Yet despite this opposition on the part of
man, God can and does come into immediate
contact with souls. Nevertheless it is still
true that the normal and regular channel
of His action is the Church, the mistress of
truth and dispensatrix of His graces. In
her official teaching, she can, and she should
insist on this providential economy. Is it
not necessary, then, that she preach Jesus
and bring to the fore the means of salvation
which He himself has prescribed? This becomes the more incumbent upon her in order
to rouse the indifferent into action and to
counteract the purely natural tendency which
claims that man has a right to formulate his
own religious beliefs, or that he is justified
in choosing at his pleasure any one of the
rival religions of the world. After all, her

preaching along these lines is the truth, viewed, so to speak, in the very intention of God and in the revelation of His will to us.

This solution, founded on the distinction between the ordinary Providence of God, which He has revealed to us, and His extraordinary Providence whereby He mysteriously supplies the weakness and overcomes the opposition arising from secondary causes, is fully justified by the data of the problem. We must understand our axiom in the sense of referring to the *per se,* not to the *per accidens;* to the general economy, and not to individual souls.

We cannot be accused of suppressing half the truth, nor can we be charged with being mistaken in regard to facts. There is a closer connection between what we term the ordinary economy of salvation and the general Providence of God manifested towards humanity, than is apparent at first sight. In actual life, how many there are who live in the Church and by the Church, who live on the truth which she teaches and share in the graces of which she is the depository, without realizing at all what they owe her! All who are baptized, are, so to speak, baptized

Catholics, for baptism is the rite of entrance into the true Church, not into the dissenting sects.   Hence, all who are baptized, whether they are heretics or schismatics, provided they do not sin against the light, will continue to be indebted to the true Church for the graces which God has bestowed upon them through the instruction they have received, the ceremonies in which they participate, and the sacraments of which they can be the recipients in their particular sect.   Because it preserves the teaching of the true Church, this doctrine is the same doctrine which she received from her Founder, and it is the one which she still imparts to her children. True, in passing through purely human channels — that is, through the preaching of heretical doctrines — it does not remain untarnished, for it is mixed with error; but whatever pure and whatever good is derived from the sects comes from the divine source and through the Church.   Other things being equal, the same may be said of the liturgical life and the sacraments.[2]

[2] St. Augustine often expressed the same thought in the Donatist controversy. He writes to Vincentius: "From the Catholic Church are all the

Who can tell how far those unbelievers who attain a knowledge of the truth necessary for salvation and acquire the virtue of charity, are unconsciously indebted to the light of the Church and to her mysterious influence? Leaving aside the many prayers which ascend to heaven to bring down the grace of God upon the world, do we not find the whole world saturated, as it were, with Christian ideas, filled, so to speak, with the spirit which through the mystic body of Christ makes felt the mysterious whisperings from on high, so much so that the souls possessing it know neither whence it cometh nor whither it goeth? I have said that it emanates from the Church; but it also leads the souls who correspond to it, back to the Church. For by participation in revealed truth and by sharing in the divine life, these souls are fashioned by God for the Church. Should it happen that they come into contact with her, in their journey towards eternal happiness, they will recognize her, by I know

sacraments of the Lord," even among the schismatics and heretics who departed from Holy Mother the Church and took those sacraments with them. See the whole text in Letter xciii, no. 46.

not what mysterious affinity between the
life of the Spirit within themselves and the
life of the Spirit which is in the Church.
Should it happen that they never come in
touch with her, they tend towards a meet-
ing point, viz., the end of their earthly
lives, when they will receive in her and
through her, the fulness of Christ living in
His mystical body.   All these souls belong
then in some fashion to the Church, in this,
namely, that the graces they receive are due
to the merits of Christ, the mystical head of
the Church and flow, as it were, from the
grand current issuing from the Head to His
members in His mystical body.   Then, too,
they receive these graces as pledges of
eventually coming, either in this world or in
the next, into living unity with this mystical
body.   They are members of the Church according to divine intention; they belong to
her at heart; and until they are incorporated
into the mystical body of Christ, either in
this world or in the next, they walk in the
light of truth and are already living her life.

Hence, the more we consider the profound
reality of things, the more we see that certain souls are members of the Church who

apparently have nothing in common with her. We have but to press this line of argument a little farther to come to the certain conclusion that not only is the Church the only society of salvation here below, but that, according to the providential order and the manifest intention of God, every soul saved belongs in some fashion to the Church, and no soul can be saved except through affiliation with her.

Certainly, the condition of those souls who live in the midst of heretics, schismatics, and infidels, is quite different from that of those who are full-fledged members of the Catholic Church. Whilst the latter, so to speak, bathe in the waters of grace and truth, the former receive, relatively speaking, but occasional droplets which with great difficulty trickle through an arid and miry soil. Yet that they might not perish in misery and hunger, God has vouchsafed to bestow upon them whatever is necessary to obtain salvation. These gifts, however, when compared to the abundance of supernatural privileges which He lavishes upon His children in His Church, are very little after all. They are the crumbs fallen from the table of the children, crumbs which the soul-hungry seize upon with eagerness.

And even these leavings, God grants them secretly, much like the father of a family would give a present to a disinherited son, whilst hiding his generosity from his other children. His manifest intention is that all men should become or re-become His children in the great house of His family, which is the Church; and He further desires that the union of all His sheep in the same sheepfold should be effected with His grace, under the guidance of the Church and through her preaching, the normal vehicles of the graces of faith and of supernatural truth. We can readily understand that the Church is moved to pity when she sees these souls seated, as it were, in the darkness and shadow of death; she knows, too, that she would fail in her mission and would betray the divine trust, were she to neglect doing everything in her power to communicate to everybody the treasures of light and truth of which she is the depository. This is why she sends her missionaries all over the world, even as Jesus sent His disciples, and as He Himself was sent by His Father. She knows full well that this apostolate of labor and prayer and sacrifice appeals strongly to the heart of God and induces Him to bestow graces more generously upon those souls who are untouched by such missionary activity. She knows, too, that in this wise and in some fashion, she becomes the mother of the children whom God has given her among the nations, although she is unconscious of having borne them in her womb. Far from abating her apostolic zeal, her motherly love for these benighted souls, which are hers by a special and mysterious action of God, impels her to procure for them, by all means in her power, that superabundant life which courses within her.

These conclusions become the clearer when we explain how these souls, who have been barred by circumstances from all knowledge of the Church, and hence from a visible entrance into the grand and unique society of salvation, are affiliated with her by invisible ties and are her members at heart. It is just here that the notion of implicit desire plays its part, completing the theological synthesis on this point, and which the explanations already given, will aid us in comprehending without difficulty.

VI

Souls affiliated with the Church unconsciously are united to her by invisible ties, for they are affiliated
with her internally, by an implicit
desire, which God is pleased to regard
as equivalent to external membership.

This distinction between union with the
Church *in act* and union *in desire* dates far
back into Christian antiquity. St. Ambrose
employed it in his treatise on Valentinian
who died a catechumen (and therefore, without the sacrament of baptism). His whole
line of argument tends to show that in his
mind Valentinian was really baptized because he had the *desire of baptism.*[1] The

[1] *De obitu Valentiniani*, n. 51–53: "But I hear
that you grieve because he did not receive the sacrament of baptism. Tell me now what else have we
if not desire and will? He in very truth had this
wish that, before he came to Italy, he should be in-

Church theologians have adopted this distinction, and St. Thomas repeatedly deduces his arguments from it, especially in those passages on baptism and the Holy Eucharist to which we have already referred. This was an implicit indication of the use to which this distinction could be put in treatises on the Church, and for centuries the application has been classical.

Theologians maintain that communion with the Church is necessary for salvation; they likewise claim that it is not necessary to be united to her in fact (*re*), but that it is sufficient to be in communion with her in desire (*voto*), if actual union is impossible.

But how explain this desire? What real-

---

itiated into the Church and immediately baptized by me. . . . Had he not then the grace which he desired so earnestly? Did he not have the grace he demanded? Certainly, for he who demands receives. Why did not he who had your spirit, receive your grace? But if it is a fact that because the sacraments are not solemnly celebrated they have no value, then the martyrs if they were only catechumens would not receive the crown of glory; for no one is crowned who is not initiated. But if people are absolved in their own blood, then this man's piety and will absolved him." Clearly, according to St. Ambrose, the desire of baptism, like martyrdom, replaces baptism of water.

ity must be given it? At first sight it appears that union with the Church in desire is impossible, for certainly no one can desire what he is ignorant of, and the souls we have in mind are supposed to be invincibly ignorant of the Church, or at least of her claims as the one and only society in which there is salvation. Of course, the idea of the divine intention and the objective reality of things of which we were speaking, come to help us. But what is the subjective part which each soul plays in order thus to enter this providential ark of salvation? Under the divine influence the soul unites its understanding to the divine truth by adhering to what is manifested to it; it unites its will to the divine will so that it desires all that God wills and earnestly seeks to fulfil all that He has ordained for salvation. In a word, it strives to act according to the lights afforded by conscience. These lights, it is true, are far from perfect, but the will reaches farther than the understanding; willing all that God wills, the soul, because of the union of will with Him, enters fully into all the divine plans and into all the divine designs. It has but one desire, and that is, to know the will of God, so that it might be translated into life. This desire, as can be easily perceived, inheres in the very act of charity itself.

Now, in the present case, this desire implies affiliation with the Church as far as it is possible. The soul who desires to live the divine life, desires at the same time to live in the normal environment in which this divine life abounds, where the influence of the Holy Spirit, as in its proper sphere of action, has full play. Implicitly, then, such a soul desires to belong to the very body of the Church. This desire, we say, is implicit, for the explicit desire would presuppose a knowledge of the Church as the unique society of salvation. But there is as much reality in this implicit desire as in the explicit desire, since the limits of the one, like those of the other, are determined exclusively by the divine will and the fidelity of the soul to that will.

Hence we see that a soul may belong to the Church in desire, without suspecting at all that there is such a thing as a Church. We must now explain the manner in which this desire may be equivalent to the reality.

This equivalence does not exist in the judgment of men, simply because the desires and yearnings of the soul are unknown to men. It immediately becomes evident to him who would know of this desire, at least as far as the essentials are concerned. Is it not this desire that we spontaneously recognise in the case of our separated brethren, for example, in the case of the Anglicans and the orthodox Russians, when we see them adhering to Christ by faith and by works of faith, yet all the while in invincible ignorance of the exclusive rights of the Roman Church? They are faithful sheep, yet they wander, unconsciously it is true, in the midst of a strange flock; but we regard them as members of the true flock of Christ because at heart, despite their errors, they are in the sheepfold of Christ. The same is the case, other things being equal, with those who live outside all visible relation with Christ or any of the Christian sects.

Still more is this true in the eyes of God. Whilst man is necessarily unable to go much beyond the surface of things, and can only judge by appearances, the divine eyes can see things as they really are, can look deep into the heart, and can search the conscience. What counts most with God is that which relates to the moral and religious order. By the religious and moral order we mean the inner disposition, namely the good will. The will, as moralists say, has both good and bad objects; but St. Thomas, with his usual clearness, explains how objects, good or evil, are such only as the specific terms of the moral act, and that, therefore, if the objects specify the acts, they enter into the moral order, to put it properly, only as the exterior terms of the interior acts which they specify.

In God's sight the value of the individual soul is measured by its interior sentiments and its good will. The exterior act itself, though not valueless in the sight of God, receives its value exclusively from the will and good intention, in so far only as it reflects the heart and soul. Hence, we can understand that affiliation or non-affiliation with the Church by visible ties and outward communion, may be to Him, if we may use the expression, something altogether secondary and unimportant. The distinction between the visible and the invisible is important only to us, since for God all is visible. Was it not St. John Chrysostom, who, I think, following Origen, said that with God the intention counts as the act?[2] This is but saying in other language what we have termed the equivalence, in the divine sight, of desire and reality.

We can truly count as members of the Church all those who are united to God in faith and charity in a degree sufficient to secure their salvation. Such membership does not result necessarily from this union of faith and charity, but it does as a matter of fact in the present order, by the conformity it establishes between the human will and the divine will, God having ordained that in the present order the Church should be the unique society of salvation, even if He does not demand as a condition of salvation outward and visible affiliation with the Church, which often depends on the free influence of human causes and outward circumstances,

[2] This is also the thought of St. Ambrose in the text cited above. But it is not expressed with the same precision. St. Bernard has uttered it in his striking formula: "What is clearer than that the will is taken for the act, when the act is excluded by necessity?" *De baptismo* c. 2, no. 8.

from which He does not intend to exempt His elect scattered throughout the world, in order to place them visibly in the one sheepfold of Christ.

From the fact that God forges, by some mysterious process, the invisible ties by which all souls of good faith and good will, and those faithful to divine grace are united to the Church, we are forced again to conclude, what we have fully shown by the positive texts of Scripture adduced in the early part of our study, that this affiliation, far from being a side or secondary consideration for these souls, is on the contrary a matter of life and death. As a matter of fact, God does not forge these invisible binding links except and in virtue of the efforts of each soul to unite itself visibly to Him. Far from basing any conclusion against the necessity of visible affiliation upon this doctrine of invisible membership, we must on the contrary, make it a starting point in order to get a better understanding of the practical necessity incumbent upon each soul confronted with this problem, of seeking out the true Church of Christ, and of adhering to it once it has been found.

Hence, although we can say with equal truth, either that these souls belong to the Church, or that they do not belong to it, it must be admitted, taking into account the nature of things and the inmost sentiments of these souls, that they belong to it (at least at heart), since without being affiliated with her by ties visible to human sight, they are united to her by bonds visible to the divine eye. To be part of the mystical body of Christ is to be in His visible Church.

Consequently, although it may be truly said that there have been souls who have gained salvation outside the Church, we cannot say, because of this fact, that salvation is equally possible for those without as well as for those within the Church, since those very souls who are saved outside the Church (that is, without being, properly speaking, members of the visible Church) are not saved except by the Church and in so far as they are her members.

VII

Why the Church continues to preach this doctrine and why she still maintains this axiom. How she depends on her theologians to explain and defend it, without any pretence of being the last court of appeal regarding the secret workings of God. How this doctrine, far from detracting from her charity, broadens and stimulates her to bring the scattered sheep into the sheepfold.

After this brief outline, we can understand why the Church, in spite of the objections raised by those who are ignorant or impervious to divine wisdom, has calmly persisted not only in teaching but also in demanding that her children accept as an article of faith the ancient formula, "Outside the Church there is no salvation." Were she to let go unchallenged and unrefuted the statement

that any one can be saved, whether affiliated
with the Church or not, she would by that
very indulgence nullify one of the truths of
revelation, namely, the establishment of the
Church by Christ as the one and only society
necessary for salvation. Nay more, she
would, by her acquiescence, vitiate the real
sense of many Biblical passages and traditional faith formulas, in all of which this
same divine purpose is clearly enunciated.
The change produced in the world's history
by the advent of Christ would disappear and
the expectations of faith with it. It still
could be said that there is no salvation without Jesus, and even such an assertion would
give rise to the same difficulties and would
necessitate the very same distinctions as are
demanded by the parallel assertion, " Outside
the Church there is no salvation." But then
there would be no meaning to St. John's
statement that Jesus was to die in order " to
gather together in one the children of God
that were dispersed." [1] There would be
no meaning to Christ's own declaration:
" Other sheep I have, that are not of this
fold: them also must I bring, and they shall

[1] John XI. 52.

hear my voice, and there shall be one fold and one shepherd."[2] There would be no meaning in the forcible expression of St. Cyprian that " no one can have God for his Father, who has not the Church for his mother "; nor in the many formulas in which the Church is represented as the mother of souls; nor in the expressive language of St. Irenæus in regard to the Church, which he depicts as the repository of the riches of Christ; nor in his pregnant statement that wherever the Church is, there is the Spirit of God. Then, too, all the teaching of Jesus in regard to the necessity of baptism, the power conferred upon the Apostles of forgiving sins, the necessity of believing the Gospel preaching under the pain of damnation, would either have to be rejected as unauthentic, or their obvious meaning distorted or denied.

The Church is obliged, as long as she desires to keep intact the edifice of Christian truth, of which she is, according to St. Paul, the pillar and the ground, to profess and to impose on our belief the dogma which finds its best expression in the celebrated phrase,

[2] John X. 16.

" Outside the Church there is no salvation."
Further, she depends upon her theologians
and her apologists to explain it in its real
meaning and to place it in its true light.   To
them she leaves the task of showing that in
proclaiming this truth she does not contra-
dict herself and at the same time, that she
has never ceased to profess that no one is
damned except through his own fault and
that God includes among His children, even
now, throughout the entire world, souls who
belong to Him and live His life, without any
visible affiliation with her and without any
reception of the divine life through the ordinary channels of the Gospel preaching and
the sacraments.

Yet side by side with her confidence that
her theologians will furnish the necessary
explanations, that they will systematize her
doctrine, and will answer all the objections
it may occasion, the Church is fully conscious
of, and recognizes, the mysterious influence
of God on the conduct of individual souls,
and she refers us to heaven for the answer
to all our difficulties on this score.   This is
just what Pius IX has done in the documents
so often referred to in the course of this

study. " Far be it from us," he says, " to be so rash as to fix limits to the mercy of God, which is infinite; far be it from us to endeavor to sound the depths of the mysterious designs of God and His judgments, which are unfathomable. . . . When freed from the bonds of our bodies, we shall see God as He is, we shall no doubt know how close and admirable is the bond which unites divine justice to divine mercy." [3]

" Here below let us firmly believe what God teaches us, and distrust the false teachings which tend to foster this religious indifference, which is ruinous to souls." And " as charity demands, let us pray ceaselessly that the entire world may be converted to Christ, and let us labor as hard as we possibly can for the salvation of all men, assured of the fact that the arm of God is not shortened and that the gifts of heavenly grace are not wanting to those who with a sincere heart desire and ask for this beneficent light." [4] We have been accused " of being the enemies of those who are not bound to us by the ties

[3] In the allocution *Singulari quadam,* Dec. 9, 1854. EDB 1646–1647.

[4] *Ibid.,* 1648.

of the same faith and charity." But this is a calumny, pure and simple. We pity them and are ready "to render them all the services of Christian charity"; we are ready especially "to leave nothing undone to bring them from the darkness of error, in which they are sunken, into the Church, their all-loving mother, who never ceases to extend her arms to them in maternal love and to call them back to her bosom, so that, grounded and strengthened in faith, hope, and charity, and fructifying in every good work, they may attain to eternal salvation." [5]

[5] Encyclical *Quanto conficiamur moerore,* Aug. 10, 1863. EDB 1678.

THE END

Available wherever Catholic books are sold.

Available wherever Catholic books are sold.